Frantz Fanon was in the United States from October 23 to December 6 1961. He was housed at the Dupont Plaza (now Dupont Circle) Hotel in Washington, DC until October 30th and then moved to the National Institute of Health in Bethesda, MD, where he died on December 6.

Frantz Fanon in the United States

Christian Filostrat

Published by PIERRE KROFT LEGACY PUBLISHERS,
2022.

Frantz Fanon in the U.S.

Followed by comments from Josie Fanon, his wife

by Christian Filostrat

PIERRE KROFT LEGACY PUBLISHERS 4075 Jefferson Parkway, Lake Oswego, OR 97035

USA

Library of Congress Publication Data Filostrat, Christian *Fanon in the U.S.*

Cataloguing-in- Library of Congress

TO JOSIE FANON

For her contributions and sacrifices

/

À Josie Fanon

Pour ses contributions et ses sacrifices

ABOUT THE AUTHOR

Christian Filostrat is a Senior America diplomat, a graduate of the National War College, a 1994 Presidential Award recipient, and the author of *The Secret of the Dictator* a novel about political relations between the United States and the Democratic Republic of the Congo. *Containing China* is book one of his Congo trilogy, a novel about an American intervention in a papal election involving a Congolese cardinal. The tale of the Catholic Church in the Congo after WWII is told in *If not you, Who,* completing the trilogy.

Négritude The Origin is a scholarly work by Christian Filostrat based on the newspaper, *L'Etudiant Noir*, and Aimé Césaire's article, *Racial Consciousness and Social Revolution,* which launched the Négritude movement in Paris in 1935.

*Frantz Fanon in the United States:*On his deathbed, the humanist–anti-colonialist assesses his struggle against colonialism, with comments from his wife, Josie Fanon.

QUOTATION PAGE

National liberation is the first step. Without independence, nation building cannot begin. Josie Fanon

Colonialism is like a religion. This is why the colonialist wants the subjugated to accept their condition at all costs. Unless the natives claim their personal inferiority and that of their culture, they are considered disloyal inferiors. You are dominated because you are inferior. You have to accept it. You have to show it. It is that simple. There is no reverse of this coin.

But the hard facts were that fifty years of non-violence had brought the African people nothing but more and more repressive legislation, and fewer and fewer rights. Nelson Mandela

If all the Arabs and Berbers in Algeria are considered French My village will no longer be called Colombey-les-Deux-Églises but Colombey-les-Deux-Mosquées. Charles de Gaulle

The Algerians have been subjected to enough humiliation, racism and ill treatment for more than a century. They wanted full citizenship in a country of their own. That is why they wanted independence. Qurah

We revolt because, for many reasons, we can no longer breathe. Frantz Fanon

The 'French fact' cannot be eliminated in Algeria, and the dream of a sudden disappearance of France is childish. Albert Camus.

This Wampanoag tribe helped the Pilgrims survive their first Thanksgiving. They still regret it 400 years later.

AUTHOR'S NOTE

I relied more on conversations and interviews with people who frequently visited Fanon than I did on his books and the articles he wrote for El Moudjahid. Of course, his wife. She was with him in Bethesda, Maryland until the end. She is the primary source of information. (From her, I was able to discover how highly Fanon regarded the participation of women in the Algerian Revolution, as well as how much of an impact his upbringing in colonial Martinique had on the revolutionary ideals and actions he took during his adult life.) Bertene Juminer, a Guyanese physician and writer, was with Fanon in Tunisia and had a lot to say about Fanon's worldview and work based on conversations he and others had with him. We talked about Fanon for days in Cayenne. Leon Damas, who was in Rome at the time of Fanon's meeting with Jean Paul Sartre and Simone de Beauvoir.

Joby Fanon, his brother, wrote an excellent biography of him. Aimé Césaire described the socio-political climate in Martinique when Fanon was his student at the Lycée Victor Schelcher in Fort de France in 1942. There were others. I regret not speaking with Leopold S. Senghor about Fanon's offer to work in Senegal when I was in Dakar. Given his views on Algeria, it would have been interesting to talk with Senghor about Fanon and the revolution.

Senghor meant it when he said, "I have a great weakness for France." He wasn't kidding. He worshiped France, and as if to sanctify himself, he practiced the cult of France. It was like an illness. I could never meet him without marveling at the Frenchness he exuded, no matter how many times I saw him. It's as though he couldn't wait to show how much France meant to him. When it came to France, he was just like a kid. (It's worth noting that Senghor, the agrégé de grammaire, a degree as difficult to obtain in France as a medical degree, spoke French with his native Senegalese Serer accent, rather than the Negro-de-Paris

French accent that others from the colonies adopt after a visit to Paris, which Fanon found alienating.) You might wonder how an African leader with a degree in French grammar can benefit his country. Senghor was going to teach French in French lycées. But he was too good to be true for Paris to overlook him as its most loyal agent in Ouest Africa. France was exceptionally fond of loyal évolués. Unsurprisingly members of the Académie Française elected him a member shortly after he left office.

My take on Senghor and Algeria is shaped by a meeting with Senghor in 1983, when I was the Cultural Attaché at the US Embassy in Dakar. Randall Robinson of Trans-Africa was in town, and I arranged an interview with him for Dakar's daily, Le Soleil. The Western Sahara issue was one of the topics discussed. Robinson expressed his support for the Sahrawi people and the Polisario Front. The interview was never published. President Senghor, on the other hand, summoned me to his office.

This time it was a furious Senghor I was meeting. He informed me that he could not let views in the Senegalese media that were hostile to Morocco's interests. He then proceeded to give me a full lesson on Arab racism, with the exception of Morocco.

The fact that Mauritania, a slave state over the Senegal River, insisted on an Arab appellation didn't help matters. He grew bitter. Senghor was one of the most guarded persons I'd ever met, so I was taken aback. But, possibly because he was only a few months away from announcing his retirement, he let it all hang out here.

According to his wife, Fanon spoke intermittently but vehemently in his hospital bed. Everything was on the line. I utilized a series of paragraphs to show how he presented himself in that situation.

I am solely responsible for any inaccuracies.

I got a feeling for what kind of man Fanon was from listening to his voice on audio recordings. I noticed his tremendous concentration. Also, perhaps he was disciplined but impatient. I must agree that hearing him speak on Houphouet-Boigny, for example, was eye opening.

U.S. INTELLIGENCE SERVICES (CIA) AND FRANTZ FANON

Through the good offices of the government of Tunisia, the C.I.A. (C. Oliver Iselin III, 1927-2017) escorted Frantz Fanon to the United States (and his remains back to Tunisia). They arrived at Idlewild Airport (now JFK) on Monday, October 23 1961. Fanon first went to Moscow for treatment, but was told that NIH was the pre- eminent institution for his leukemia. He is thirty- six years old.

American intelligence services had no reason to assist an unrelenting anti-imperialist Algerian revolutionary who was near death and had nothing of value to offer in exchange for assistance. The cold war is the key to making sense of why they did. It's 1961. An American invasion attempt just ended in failure at the Bay of Pigs in Cuba. The Cuban Missile Crisis will endanger the entire world in less than a year. The United States was courting strategically located Algeria, which had effectively defeated France in its Revolution, by providing medical care to Fanon, who was deathly ill, in case the Algerians were needed again in the near future. (Recall that the US landed to liberate Europe from the Nazis on November 8, 1942. Landing on three Algerian beaches - two west of Algiers and one east - started the invasion. U.S. Army Infantry Division Major General Charles W. Ryder led the landing forces. Algeria would again be strategic if the US had to send troops back to Europe to stop a Soviet invasion.)

Room 37, National Institute of Health, Maryland, USA, December 5, 1961. A dying 36-year-old revolutionary reflects on hisjourney and the certainties he found along the way.

White blood cells, like invading colonial settlers, displace the erythrocytes that give me oxygen. I have acute lymphoid leukemia.

Life revolves around me like a dragonfly without wings. I recently lived without reservation or hindrance. By whose sleight of hand is life now a dragonfly without wings? In the victory parade down Avenue Didouche Mourad, I would have liked to see the sky lit up in my eyes. I cling tenaciously to the meaning of life, not thinking about death before the revolution's official triumph.

As if battling colonialism, I use my impending death to focus on what I've gone through over the years. The threat of death is a one-of-a-kind motivator. It compels me to investigate my hallucinations, and as I do so, the events of my life race through my head like a crazed horse. I'm back on the battlefield, reflecting on my journey and my convictions. Hopes, despair, and fatigue have all been intertwined with cell counts since October. In the case of the fever, it's a game of hide and seek with the chill, and it takes me back to my childhood in Martinique before the war. We were obsessed with playing hide and seek, especially at night.

Another pastime was playing outlaw (coups de bandits). The adults watched us from their doors and whispered to us safe places to hide. René was usually the most whispered to. He spoke French with a Negro-de-Paris accent, indicating that he had visited France. Because of this, the adults favored him. We didn't think much of it. We even thought it was appropriate because he had visited France and touched French soil. Colonialism, which was not conditional but entirely racial, was binding, and France represented the pinnacle of our existence.

It's as if two powerful kingdoms agreed that the fever would come at night and the chills would come during the day. This arrangement has nothing to do with me. As I told my wife Josie at the start of my night shivers in Tunisia, this is happening without any personal input. Because I was afraid of the dark as a child, I believe that stress causes the fever to burn more eagerly after dark.

"When did you decide to become a revolutionary?" Josie was curious. I told her in Caribbean Creole, without hesitation and cynically, to be funny, but above all to emphasize that Martinique shaped who and what I am. But she didn't understand me; she doesn't speak my native tongue.

According to Albert Camus, football is responsible for everything in his life. Martinique is responsible for everything in mine. I wouldn't be who I am today if I hadn't grown up in Martinique. In short, my character was shaped by French colonialism. Then my wife asked, "What would you be if you weren't a revolutionary?" I didn't have an answer. I couldn't imagine myself as anything other than an anti-colonialist revolutionary. I use French-Caribbean Creole when I'm delirious. I'm not sure why my subconscious insists on using Creole. I can clearly hear myself, but I have no control over my thoughts or how they are expressed.

As a result, I believe those who brought me here installed a Creole speaker in my room to monitor my episodic delirium. He's taking notes. They also had someone at the Washington Hotel, where I was detained for a week. I'm aware that they'll require a piece of my skin in exchange for my medical treatment at this prestigious hospital. (Being a friend of Roberto Holden, an American agent, also helped.) Whatever America's position on the Algerian revolution, a cold war is raging, and France, as a NATO member, expects some consideration. You're wasting your time; delirium is incoherent, and you're ranting in your head rather than out loud. That's one reason torture is a waste of time.

My patients at Blida told me a lot more when they were coherent than when they were raving.

In my delirium, what could I possibly tell them that they didn't already know? That there is no occupation without violence? That violence is the mode of communication between colonizers and colonized, oppressor and oppressed? They know this.

Colonialism is grounded in racism and the belief that Arabs, blacks, slaves, the abused, and the colonized are members of inferior sub-human races, somewhere between animal and human, doomed to exploitation and without the ability to resist colonial occupation.

Algerian settlers believed that natives were created for their occupation. It was biologically required. Although wishful thinking is dangerous, it has been a feature of France's colonial mission in Algeria for the past 130 years.

Underestimating the natives:

The settlers invent a colonial Algeria where the inhabitants are caricatured based on the settler's wants and needs. Algerians are portrayed as subordinate Arabs, apolitical masses who are naturally submissive and docile. A settler's mind is a marvel of candor, pathologically incapable of not underestimating the indigène. This mindset traps the settlers in their own traditions and colonial temperament. I can see the clinical reasoning behind this. Just as I understand that the indigène eventually succumbs to the obligation to breathe, much like a gravitational force imposed on him. In the end, that force triumphs over all fears. Even a mouse can become enraged. There's also the pathology of the indigène in search of what he is.

The settler does not even pause for a moment to consider that he may be mistaken about the natives. His identity and interests are dependent on exploiting the Algerians, hence his dismissive attitude toward them. The idea that the natives may develop a natural animosity toward the settlers is one that the settlers rarely consider. It seems that because of who they are, they are unable to even fathom doing something like that. The colonial occupier's limited perspective on the world is one of the most significant psychological obstacles he faces.

How do the oppression and exploitation of indigenous people be rationalized by white settlers? The following is always the justification given: "It is not possible for the locals to govern themselves. And it goes without saying that they are immoral and inferior."

Suffocated by the mediocrity of his colonial fate, the native regains his breath and his soul via aggression against the occupier.

Violence purifies on an individual level. It cures the native's inferiority complex, as well as his meditative or despondent outlook.

Violence gives him confidence and rehabilitates him in his own eyes. No one is higher than him. He regains his dignity through violence. There's no greater satisfaction than recovering independence through revolutionary liberation. The settlers are blind to their own strength and never consider being challenged. Being underestimated was Algeria's most loyal partner.

Memory is linked to speech, and language is malleable. I appreciate the scientific rationale for recalling childhood memories during delirium. I never expected that to happen to me. (Neither did I expect to die in an American hospital in 1961. Age 36.)

Finally, I don't mind that my thoughts are on Martinique - on my carefree childhood. The man staring at me must be from Martinique. I noticed him smiling. When I saw that smile, I may have unconsciously clammed up. But I'm not certain. I have periods of clarity, typically during the day, when it's the chill's turn to afflict me. These times allow me to reflect on my journey and what the Algerian revolution meant to me. Marseille, Lyon, Tunis, Rome, Paris, Blida, and the other cities I've seen feel like extensions of my youth and Martinique's colonial culture.

Even when I have a clear mind and am thinking in French, I recall my childhood and Martinique. My palliative treatment for this terminal illness allows me to dissect everything that has happened to me using an unexpectedly logical framework.

Self-definition is a gratifying act, and this yearning for life, with its end-of-life nostalgia, has me craving my mother's spicy red fish court bouillon. The only thing that's bad about this place is the food.

The cancer cell count, like the fever and chill, has brought back memories. As though these cells were the provocateur in my end-of-life story. They prompt me as if on cue. It's a sign that the end is near: Memories are for when one's time is up.

As I've mentioned before, Sartre, like in so many other areas, set me on the path of thinking that it's the totality of one's life, the sum of everything one has done from A to Z. Finally, you can write your life's story. Not before. I'm there! Or, in the words of Simone de Beauvoir, "the only thing I'm not is dead."

My sight returned last night, albeit dimly, but I could see. My restored sight provided me with the kind of relief that only a reprieve from death can provide. It was as if the hospital director had personally come in to inform me that I was going to live and that a cure for my leukemia cell counts was on the way. I was expected to march in the Revolution victory parade. After that, I was going to resume my psychiatric practice. I was going to finish the books that I needed to finish. My concerns about colonialism would be heard all over the world. That took a while to sink in, but once it did, I surrendered to the fairytale. The excitement levied a heavy tax, however. I paid by falling asleep without help from any capsule. However, the fever could not be fooled and did not forgo its rendezvous with my death.

Last night's fever took me back to when I was ten years old, to the day in 1935 when my uncle arrived from Le Havre on the ocean liner Colombie. He'd brought a copy of *L'Étudiant noir*, a newspaper he'd picked up in Paris. He came to see us, it seems, less to reconnect after two years in France than to talk about Aimé Césaire, the newspaper's editor, whom he had met in Paris. He was overjoyed that Césaire's best friend was Pierre Aliker, André Aliker's younger brother. That piqued my parents' interest as well. I was also curious because the previous year, in January,

I had joined my brothers to Fond Bourlet to see André Aliker's body washed up on the beach, tied from head to toe. Everyone in Martinique was there to gawk, since it was the body of someone they all knew. That had never happened before in my memory. It was the first actual sensation I'd ever had in my life. I also recall that no one on the beach doubted that a béké settler, whose wife Aliker had accused of tax evasion in his publication *Justice*, had murdered him. In Martinique, *Justice* was the Communist Party's press organ.

The French colonials, descendants of the slave owners, were known as békés. They controlled the island's economy. But we rarely saw them. There was no one who could tell you how many there were. They resided within walls, overlooking the sea. My siblings and I tossed rocks at their mango trees, but the fences kept us from getting any. My education in the Master-Bondsman Dialectic began with firsthand experiences, such as the béké's murder of André Aliker on January 12, 1934. The béké master once again demonstrated what happens to bondsmen who violate their status.

To be clear, the béké killed Aliker for more than just opposing his wife; he killed him for exceeding his bondsman status. Aliker was a "traitor" to the békés for joining the Communist Party, a French group hostile to the béké class's dominance over Martinique. Joining the Communist Party was also a liberated act that the békés could not tolerate. Even if the communists sought merely social adjustment rather than independence, it was plenty to worry the békés, who, as tense as a mongoose in heat, spent a significant amount of time keeping an eye out for any natives who demanded a change in the way things were.

Any mention of reparation or wealth redistribution was deemed reprehensible and condemned.

In terms of my education, the communists then represented a France antagonistic to the békés, much like the France of the French Revolution. I had aspired to be a poet and a playwright, but in January 1934, I aspired to be a revolutionary. I had no idea it would be Algeria, a stopover during the war that would turn me into one. Twenty years later, Algerian békés put a price on my head, just as Martinique békés did on Aliker's, Belgians on Lumumba's, and the French on Moumié's. They would have given anything to get rid of what I represented. Brutality is the preferred way of communication among békés worldwide. As well as being expedient, brutality is intimate and embraces all the human emotions. Moreover, békés believe that brutality maintains indigenous people in lockstep with the colonial arrangement and the continuation of the occupation.

Césaire's friendship with Aliker made him a champion of the working class. One of the mothers of future French West Indian tragedies was hidden in this seemingly innocuous story. Césaire and I met a few years later when I attended high school at the Lycée Victor Schoelcher, which overlooks the Bay of Fort de France. "I'm a Marxist," he explained.

No one was as gifted, charismatic, or distant as Césaire. Also noteworthy: He never spoke a single word in the native tongue. He could only communicate in French. What a French! I'm not sure who said it, but I believe it was a French state minister: "When Césaire speaks, French grammar smiles." The people in the countryside had no idea what he was saying. His accent, on the other hand, made it clear that he'd been to France and that his French was unlike any other. Césaire and his vision of who he and his people were and on whom they depended had complete control of the political pitch. Césaire pushed for the island to stay under French occupation, dooming it to a colonial future where, in my opinion, it is worse to live than to die.

My father read from *L'Étudiant noir*, which my uncle had brought with him. "He is no communist," he declared after reading Césaire's editorial. Césaire's compelling writing, in reality, shouted out against the communists' social aspirations. Césaire was promoting racial consciousness. He dubbed that Négritude. Césaire had a gift with words. He was a master *di bella parole*, as the Italians put it. I could spend all day listening to him speak in his unique fricative style. He urged Martinique to acknowledge their black race, embrace their Négritude heritage, to highlight that blacks were not white Frenchmen.

That was even less appealing in 1935 than what the communists were advocating. Can you picture folks exclaiming how happy they were to be black? Césaire didn't elaborate on how they planned to make that leap. It appeared that racial consciousness would be an end in itself, rather than a dialectical evolution. It would not, for example, be a step toward ending the béké settler's dominance of Martinique. However, blacks couldn't be anything other than black, and they had to accept that truth. Was this to be a stepping-stone on the path to liberation? That's what I assumed. So I agreed with Césaire when he recommended accepting our black destiny, history, and culture ... until I realized there was no national liberation in what he was proposing.

Négritude was in fact an obstacle to national liberation. As Césaire advocated for the continuation of the French occupation, there was no escape route for a black destiny outside of French domination. The main goal of his proposal was to oppose France's colonial deculturation / assimilation agenda. Négritude was opposed to assimilation in order to keep Martinique's black element consciously black, but only in order to make Martiniquans full partners in the French colonial enterprise. For the black man there would be only one destiny. And it was to be colonized French. In the end, Césaire was offering blacks a union with colonialism. When I realized this, it seemed too unbelievable to be imagined.

The French Empire was made up of a variety of colored peoples. If blacks accepted the reality of their Négritude, they would be rightly distinguished from other groups of assimilated natives and would no longer be seen as simply another group of natives of lower social status. They'd no longer be subordinates. They would be France's partners in the empire. Négritude would have gained blacks comprehensive rights in addition to legitimacy, and they would have a legitimate seat at the empire's whimsical "give and take" table. (Proponents of this scenario, Césaire and his junior partner, Senghor, had a particular fondness for the expression *la table du donné et du recevoir* – the give and take table.) It was one of their Négritude's favorite catchphrases. They wore it out. They would be the black partners in the French empire, no longer accommodating natives, at that fanciful table. (There couldn't be room for any national liberation in all of this.)

What makes it too fantastic to be imagined is that Césaire (Senghor followed Césaire) did not take into account the space between the colonizer and the colonized, the dominant and the dominated. Otherwise, he would have been on top of the folly of the French colonizer giving the natives a socio-political alternative outside of colonialism's parameters. But those brilliant men did envision that scenario and would have gone to any length to make it a reality. Exasperated, de Gaulle reminded Senghor that the French were "a European people of the white race, of Greek and Latin culture and of the Christian religion." Even so, Senghor's worship of France never dimmed - it remained a cult.

(They were not Négritude advocates but assimilated *colonisés* – *évolués* – natives who had undergone an evolution from their forebears' African origin. More than any others, Martiniquan *évolués* served in France's colonial empire's highest official positions. They were the classic empires' auxiliaries. A favorite of General de Gaulle, Guyanese Félix Éboué is the most prominent assimilated *colonisés* to have held high colonial offices – Guadeloupe's governor in1936 and governor general of the entire French East Africa from 1940 until 1944. He lies in France's Pantheon. Leopold S. Senghor married his daughter Ginette.) Speaking of France's Pantheon, I wouldn't be surprised if Aimé Césaire and Leopold Senghor didn't end up there as well. Such loyal *évolués,* enthusiasts of French colonialism, deserve no less. And that would be yet another propaganda coup France couldn't pass up.

There is no mystery to colonialism: "The colony was established for the benefit of France." That's the injunction since the beginning. The colonialist creed does not exist in a more formalized or established state. Over the centuries, France made adjustments to fit different times and authorities, but the imperative never changed from its essence. (These days, you'll still see bronze statues of Pierre Belain d'Esnambuc, who founded the colony, adorn towns and villages.)

The colonial system may have been successful due to its force and cunning but its over-reliance on violence meant that it lacked imagination That's always been obvious to me.

Despite the fact that Césaire was familiar with the master-slave dialectic in Hegel's Phenomenology of Spirit, what was more significant to him was his belief that Martiniquans could not survive without their French overseer. Césaire surrendered to French colonialism and aspired to be French. A black Frenchman, a second-class citizen, – even within the Communist Party – but French nonetheless. It was in this context that he wrote the masterpieces of anti- colonialism that are *Discourse on Colonialism* and *Letter to Maurice Thorez*. There is no contradiction. Keep in mind that the term "كيف assimilation" refers to the same thing as "French colonialism." Césaire was opposed to كيف assimilation, but he wanted to live under French rule. He wanted his cake and eat it too (It would be a neat trick for France to have colonization without assimilation.) Césaire is most known as a poet and playwright, writer and French anti-assimilationist intellectual from Martinique. Just as I am an Algerian revolutionary born in Martinique. It is important to keep in mind that he wrote against colonialism in his capacity as a French poet and playwright, who also happened to be an anti-assimilation French intellectual. He did not write against colonialism as a black man living under French occupation yearning for liberation. That makes no sense to me at all, especially when you consider that Césaire complained constently about being colonized, even inside the Communist Party, when he was a member.

It is still possible that the people might have contemplated shutting the door on colonialism had someone as revered as Césaire promoted liberation. For such a task Césaire (even directed by the Communist Party) would've needed some audacity and plenty of conviction. I am certain the burden of advocating national liberation constrained him. Had he recused himself due to what he witnessed in Haiti?

For a variety of reasons, Césaire refused to rebel against French colonial rule. Except for the fact that the die was cast for Martinique, I believe his stay in Haiti with his wife in 1944 had something to do with it. I say this only because I can't figure out why he wanted to remain a second class citizen of France. Then too, the North Americans had occupied Haiti for 20 years and continued to threaten the Caribbean because of the war. Martinique, he probably thought, would be as mutilated as Haiti if not for France's protectorate. Martinique another Haiti! This was a nightmare he may have had.

Let us remember that apart from his anti-assimilation essays, he was not a revolutionary. In fact, he possessed no trace of a revolutionary spirit. From what I have seen, by practicing "the ethics of acceptance" Césaire is happy to be under French occupation. Fatalist certainly, but what would you do if you were not a revolutionary? You would beg at your occupier's capital's gates. You are a "native", after all, a second-class "citizen", like any colonized person. Even the alternatives available to you are those approved by your colonizer. You would borrow. You would do what you could for the people behind you. If you are not a revolutionary, the sky is limited to what your colonizer prescribes.

And since you cannot simply disappear, you affirm, even when Ibrahim Frantz Fanon denounces you, that you are proud of something - the sea which surrounds you, the sky, your race, the mountains, etc.

There was another side to Césaire I had never noticed in high school in 1942. To the few calls for independence, he responds by evoking the massacres that French troops would come to commit in Martinique in the event of an insurrection. He warned: "Independence cannot be given, it is taken, it is torn off. Independence is paid for in blood and corpses!" The ambiguous politician Césaire became was not above using the Algerian experience as a scarecrow to scare crowds back home in Martinique. He did not hesitate to issue alarmist and dishonest warnings to panic potential pro-independence voters. He was dishonest because the very last thing Martinique had to fear was an independence movement. An army of Shamans would be required for Martinique to break the colonial chains and stop being colonially fucked by France. That's why I've never returned to Martinique.

(In Martinique, I'd observe people boarding the transatlantic ocean liner Colombie for the journey to Le Havre. When they go to France, they put on airs and act like grandees. And the people on the dock watched as the island's royalty, kings and queens, boarded the ship bound for France. When they return, they don't speak in their native language. They can be identified by their newly acquired accent, the embroidered Negro de Paris. It's them in *Black Skin White Mask*.)

It makes me shudder to think that if not for the Algerian Revolution, Frantz Fanon would have been stuck in Nègritude, a peddler of a literature reconciled to French colonial dominance. In reality, Negritude is yet another way for natives to oblige the occupation. Negritude secures colonialism. This is why de Gaulle can praise "Léopold S. Senghor and his negritude," without batting an eye.

Césaire's Négritude to keep Martinique under French rule was a tragedy. Oddly, no one has investigated the malediction of assimilation, the primary feature of French colonialism, in greater depth and with greater insight. One could compare Césaire to Algeria's Ramdane Abane. But, whereas Ramdane understood that self-determination was required to operate above colonialism and occupation, Césaire was content to write masterful anti- assimilation treatises without mentioning the occupation of our homeland and deliver awe-inspiring speeches at the French National Assembly. Until recently, though, Césaire spent his time doing what the French Communist Party told him to say. And then, he pushed Martinique and the fragments of the empire that are left, mostly small islands and French Guiana, further into France's controls.

Now, Césaire is literally on his hands and knees begging De Gaulle for crumbs for Martinique. De Gaulle seems to take satisfaction double crossing Césaire. I wouldn't put it past De Gaulle to mock Césaire with quips like, "Is begging France for crumbs part of Négritude?" The more Césaire begs the more De Gaulle screws him.

Is Césaire penning revolutionary tracts more for the benefit of others than for the people of Martinique or himself? Is this some kind of story that takes place in multiple universes? A revolution consisting solely of meaningless words is, excuse me, counterrevolutionary. A revolution is a step. No revolutionary step is taken as long as the natives do not challenge the occupation on all its fronts. If liberation is the goal, words matter.

Make no mistake: If liberation is the goal, admirable words must also be at the forefront of the necessary process of self-actualization – when admirable words are part of the historical process unfolding towards national liberation. Did the Irish, for example, not prioritize their language in their struggle for national liberation?

Others like Césaire and Martinique still struggle with the assistance of their colonial overseers. In French, they are called *les assistés* (the assisted ones.) When France gets tired of these clingers on, or when it becomes economically weary of them, it will kick them out. I said something to that effect in an El Moudjahid article two years ago.

France will have to kick them hard enough in the ass to make them grow up; Césaire could easily have done what Sékou Touré did three years ago, but Touré trusted the Guineans while Césaire had no faith Martinique could exist unassisted.

*Ontology and Negritude:*

In my experience as a revolutionary Algerian, I can tell you that in order to achieve perfect blackness, you have to free yourself from colonialism by violent resistance, which is something that Négritude cannot endorse. If you don't liberate yourself, you remain masked, serving the occupation. Négritude is a mask for the occupation.

What if is a game I love to play – a game for the mind of a dying man – born of regret and wishful thinking: What if Négritude wasn't a product of French colonialism? It would no longer be Négritude, that's true, but what if ? If Aimé Césaire, with his singular personality, linguistic genius and charisma, had positioned racial consciousness, aka Négritude, as a main advocate of national liberation, French colonialism would have been significantly different.

As it is, racial consciousness, aka Négritude, has no resonance for blacks because their lives are on hold until colonialism recognizes their existence through their struggle for liberation. As long as Négritude is bound up in the servitude of colonialism, blacks will not progress toward a liberated identity. Is racial consciousness enough for a native? The one thing I am certain of is that the only thing that can be sufficient is self- determination. Without it, one is a leaf at the mercy of the colonial wind, with or without racial consciousness, aka Négritude. When someone is subjected to colonialism, his very essence is on ice.

In his epistemology of Negritude, Aimé Césaire claims, *Negritude is the simple recognition of our blackness and the acceptance of this fact of our black fate, history, and culture.* There is no mention of black fate independent of the current colonial arrangement. It feels like black people's status is permanently settled, part of colonial France, carved in colonial stone. Bottom line: Négritude is a powerful propaganda tool in the French colonial arsenal. With both hands, France makes the most of the opportunity to demonstrate its open-mindedness, cosmopolitanism, and universality by accepting, praising, and promoting Négritude. France understands that native intellectuals who express Négritude bolster France's colonial interests.

Négritude makes no attempt to develop an epistemology of colonialism or the armed struggle against it. What about ethics, the moral principle underlying a person's actions? Isn't national liberation the moral imperative of every black movement, whether Négritude or another? In Négritude, where is the liberation? In fact, Aimé Césaire, the founder of Négritude, is in favor of keeping Martinique and the other imperial confettis under French authority, while bewailing being colonized.

If Negritude contained even a glimmer of advocating liberation, whether it be achieved through armed struggle or even a method that does not involve violence, it would have an interdict up the asses of these indigenous intellectuals so quickly that it would make a spinning top of their heads.

In terms of originality and esthetics Négritude literature is superficial, derivative of what French artists create. What the surrealists came up with, and so on. What can Lautréamont's surrealist poetry do for the people living under occupation? In short, without a liberationist stance, Négritude is "just literature," as the French say. Liberation and Négritude are, in fact, ships passing in the night.

*Négritude and literature:*

Let me say a few more words about Négritude's literature. It's a literature resigned to colonial rule. That's the first thing. As far as French settlers are concerned, it's completely safe. It does not keep them awake at night. The settlers had no interest in Doudouism or any of the other French West Indian literary currents that emerged over the years. They self-importantly referred to that literature as *a pastiche*. Imitation art is not highly regarded. Colonial settlers are unconcerned if Césaire claims that blacks never invented anything. "Hurray for those who have never invented anything," I remember reading. Or, in Senghor's words, "emotions are as black as reason is European."

Communists, on the other hand, saw ethnic identity as anti-proletarian, anti-communist and anti-social revolution. There was always that element of the unknown among the Communists: You never knew how they would value the way indigenous peoples managed their own liberation struggles. To be sure, they placed a higher value on their doctrines. The revolution did not occur; dogmatic pronouncements about it did. In Sartre's assessment, the communists acted in *bad faith*.

They were pimps (maquereau) at heart, and not just because they were opposed to the Algerian revolution. (Their rigid belief that only a socialist Europe could help free Algeria from occupation was yet another example of pointless imperialist paternalism from the left.) I don't use the word "imperialist" very often. It's far too impersonal. Too removed from the Kasbah.

To Césaire, the communists were no threat to French rule in Martinique. They spoke of "Social Revolution." They were not interested in liberation. Consequently, when, he decided to enter politics, he honored his friend Aliker by letting the communists manage his candidacy for both mayor of Fort de France and deputy to the French National Assembly and promptly facilitated the drafting of the law pushing Martinique further down the colonial nadir by making it a department of France (loi Césaire March 19, 1946) along with the other scattered islands and French Guyana, ensuring they would be under French rule in perpetuity.

With so little energy left, I spent more time with Césaire than I expected. But Césaire's Martinique is synonymous with colonialism victorious, and as an anti-colonialism revolutionary, it's impossible for me to think of colonialism, colonial occupation, etc. without looking at Césaire and his Martinique. See for yourself. Click here and take a look at how the French assimilated and occupied the people of Martinique with their colonization.

It's the land that holds the position of honor for the practice of successful colonialism.

One larger-than-life leader with national liberation paranoia can mean the difference between being freed and remaining occupied. There has never been a more important lesson in my life.

Moreover, Martinique is my native land. I assure you that there would be no revolutionary like me if it were not for Martinique which gave birth to Ibrahim Frantz Fanon. It was there that I learned that colonialism is so insidious that it transforms an entire nation under its boots into self- loathing. (Read my Black Skin, White Mask.)

The guilt of not doing more for Martinique made me think that perhaps Césaire had it right. Perhaps he understood that the gangrene of colonialism had penetrated too deeply to save the patient, and he couldn't tell the patient the truth. Say that Césaire was not opposed to a French West Indies, that he was French. Second or third class, but French nonetheless. "Practice my ethics of acceptance or disappear through immigration or other means," he would say to the patient.

The obvious solution was to end all ties to colonialism, but Césaire was so committed to the idea that French colonialism could be fixed by getting rid of its intrinsic assimilation component that he couldn't bring himself to tell his fellow countrymen that the only thing that could save them was an uprising that would eventually lead to their liberation. He could only frighten Martinique by warning that in case of insurrection the French army would come to defend the occupation by all means necessary.

The Algerian National Liberation Front and Cuba had good relations, and I requested my ambassadorship be transferred from Ghana to Cuba. Unfortunately, my illness took center stage and there were urgent priorities such as finishing *The Wretched of the Earth* and getting medical treatment. Cuba is not that far. There is no reason for me not to sail to Dominica and then cross to Martinique. I did that in reverse back in 1943. The only reason I wouldn't do so now is because I have a strong aversion to the colonial legacy of the country where I was born, which continues to get screwed over by colonialism.

It will seem odd to most people that a teenager who became an anti-colonialist revolutionary crossed the Dominican Channel in a canoe during the Second World War to go fight for France . . . and even received the Croix de Guerre for valor.

I think it had something to do with seeing a Martiniquan being thrashed by two Vichy sailors in Fort de France's great square, La Savane. The man was older with a slight build but fierce like a mongoose after a snake. As the sailors fled, the Martiniquan chased after them. It was the first time I saw anything like that. Once he had their backs, after catching them, he ravaged them with blows until the stick he picked up broke. The sight of a Martiniquan fighting back thrilled me. The fact that he spoke French with an accent, illustrating his time spent in France and the way he defended himself – that impressed me immensely and made a lasting impression on me.

But the main reason was that the French béké settlers were on the side of the fascists (as were French settlers everywhere.) Yet France was fighting the fascists. And then there was the genuine concern that Martinique would fall under the control of the United States. (At the time, we were unaware that it was propaganda from the communist party.) French public propaganda also made sure we were aware of the brutal executions of Negroes in America, the lynchings. We feared that the United States would come to Martinique and lynch us. People imagined La Savane going the way of a lynching field and they said no.

There was also Jewish persecution in Europe. All persecutions were unrestrained. This would encourage Vichy, which ruled Martinique, to abuse black people. Everyone was in danger. Imagine what they would do to blacks if they could execute Jews like that. De Gaulle's invitation to the colonies to come save the motherland from the fascists provided an immediate impetus to go fight for France.

We were labeled "dissidents" because we defied Vichy orders. We risked our lives to go join General de Gaulle in Europe's war against the fascists.

We Martiniquans were at the forefront of France's civilisatrice mission, and we were proud of our blond-haired, blue-eyed Gaul grandfathers. Vercingetorix was our school hero. We were more civilized than the other indigenous peoples. We were the first évolués. We were becoming Europeans first. I recall Julius Caesar defeating Vercingetorix at the Battle of Alesia in 52 BC. That's the only thing I remember from my lycée years.

Everyone knew that if you were from Martinique, you were more cultured than someone from Guadeloupe, for example. You were more educated; lighter skinned, and spoke French with a Negro-de-Paris accent. De Gaulle was the embodiment of the France that gave us the illusion that we were all of those things - the France that was considered to be the "good" France. Pétain represented the antithesis of everything. He was the embodiment of the France that defined us as Africans, if not the Caliban of Shakespeare.

We thought of ourselves as French. We didn't define ourselves by our skin color. During WWII, I came across a German poster that read, "There will be no dogs or Jews allowed. Not even Martiniquans." "... not even Martiniquans," I'm still puzzled by. Clearly, the Germans were mocking us. Graphically! Our fantasy was amusing. However, there was something pitiful about it. And I suddenly realized, as if by revelation, that this was the lot of the wretched of the earth. The fact that we had to be somebody's subjects was the red flag.

I remember staring at this poster for a long time *bouche bée* – with my mouth open. The Germans were unconcerned about our illusory sense of self. I wouldn't be as surprised if I had been struck by lightning at the time. To say that this poster served as a notice and had an impact on me would be an understatement.

How could the colonizer de Gaulle be superior to the colonizer Pétain in the limbic system and worldview of the natives? The bottom line is that if the "empire" had not responded to De Gaulle's call to come save the motherland, France's colonial game would have ended, and I would not have become an Algerian revolutionary. No one does the right thing under colonialism. No one is born a revolutionary or a sage.

Mayotte Capecia, one of my main characters in *Black Skin, White Mask*, must have set this up, allowing me to appreciate my dream about Martinique more before showing up in a follow-up nightmare, floating above the statue of Josephine in La Savane, to tell me how much I was wrong about my birthplace and women under the occupation. She chose my deathbed as the setting for her visitation.

After discussing our son, who is in kindergarten at Howard University in Washington, and the release of my book, *The Wretched of the Earth*, we discussed how fortunate we were that Sartre agreed to write the preface. It implies that

The *Wretched of the Earth* will be read. Understanding national liberation wars and the Algerian Revolution may benefit other anti-colonialists. Nothing could have made me happier than seeing *The Wretched of the Earth* published before I died.

We then discussed the negotiations with the French at Évian-les-Bains. My wife was adamant about not discussing it. It irritates me greatly how much we are giving away. Revolutionaries aren't negotiators; they're too eager to know what it's like to be independent and powerful. We mentioned cancer cell numbers briefly to acknowledge the obvious. Even a minor cancer has billions of cells, each of which is capable of causing malignancies.

"There is an aura of malediction surrounding Mayotte Capécia," I wrote in *Mask*, not realizing how accurate I was. In one of the strangest dreams of my life, she had returned to confront me. Mayotte Capécia was cursing me in Creole, as if she were a quimboiseuse or a djnoun casting spells. What a nightmarish scenario! Only a marabout could break the curse. I was as eager to tell my wife about my latest encounter with La Capécia as a schoolboy.

That woman was cursing me like a sailor. I had flashes of blindness, and when I realized what she was saying, I heard, *"There's more to come."*

Regaining my sight was a ruse to keep me hopeful. She then accused me of intending to curse my birthplace by hiding behind Hegel's dialectics. She yelled, *You're full of French education and no different from the other blacks with French masks you so condemn.* She then asked me what I would have been if I hadn't had a French education. How could I possibly criticize a woman like her in a book? She cried out, *Has your mother walked in my shoes?* No, I shook my head. *So, gratuitously, you chose a poor working- class woman to represent black women trying to make ends meet. Who are you to call how I survive corruption? You claim that women like me are alienated. We are, of course. Will going to La Savane and proclaiming how happy I am to be black feed my children? Remove the alienation you claim I have? My grandmother was white. What's the big deal? Deny her to pass your test? Why shouldn't I identify with her? Her kind is more capable of helping me than yours. She is on the side of the conquerors, the victorious. Those who have made a difference. Your side is moping around in defeat, begging dimes from sailors all over La Savane.*

What else can we do but accept the French colonial occupation? What are women like me supposed to do? Go hungry? What about the children? Who will feed them? The conquered? Given that Martinique is not only French, but also male-dominated, what is your treatment for Martiniquan women, doctor? So I became a laundress. It's a position available to women like me. Is it because I work as a laundress that I want to bleach my skin to look French? Someone who has never experienced hunger cannot advise someone who has on how to feed herself and her children.

Mayotte Capecia, the native archetype of colonial occupations, was not really berating me in my nightmare. It was my subconscious hiding inside a bad dream. The desire to expose it demanded that I expend whatever energy I had left once I was able to focus.

Mayotte Capecia, or my subconscious, was correct – I should have said more about women under occupation in the Muslim world and Africa. For unless women are no longer despised and marginalized as second- class citizens – beasts of burden in Africa's case – Algeria and the rest of Africa will remain like mules with their front legs tied to prevent them from wandering off. We can defeat the French occupation, but the revolution will not fulfill its promise unless social barriers are removed. Social barriers are oppressive underdevelopment levies that frustrate Algerian and African progress. It will be worse than under occupation because it will be sanctified by independence. A culture of underdevelopment, as well as a new permanent socio-religious ecosystem of poverty and backwardness, will emerge.

Mayotte Capécia was caught up in the web of colonialism, engrossed in the daily struggle for survival. There, she was subjected to all manner of colonial deprivation on fronts that we can only imagine. She was living proof that colonialism does not speak, but rather humiliates. She had no choice but to follow the path of least resistance, the path of cooperation. A better life could have been right around the corner, and she would never have known. She made the best of her situation by allowing herself to be carried wherever the occupation took her. The rest are details.

The insurgency is the only path to improving the lives of natives like Mayotte Capécia. Césaire, he interacts with de Gaulle on a regular basis. He knows what it's like to be under the colonial boot, but he accepts the boot in exchange for remaining "French." His approval is confirmed by French colonial rule. Césaire has a lot of options in life. What options and representation did Mayotte Capécia have? Mayotte Capécia, the allegory, would not recognize an option even if it were staring her in the face.

As you can see, I've learned a lot since *Black Skin, White Mask*.

I was so eager to dissect the psychological trauma caused by colonization that I neglected the Mayottes Capécias. I was so preoccupied with that psyche that I missed what was right in front of me.

The indigenous population make up Mayotte Capécia. She lives in the slums and the bidonvilles. The ragged proletariat, the outcast townspeople. As such she is critical to national liberations. In retrospect, I now understand there can be no successful uprising unless the Mayottes Capécias are involved. *They make the revolution with urban intellectuals supporting the peasantry.* We are shortchanging the revolution and doing the occupier's a service if we do not take Mayotte Capécia seriously enough to include her in the uprising.

As Nietzsche would put it, I speak about personal experiences. Everything I've ever written is based on empirical observation, on my firsthand knowledge of the forces that shaped the occupation and the forces required to defeat it. There is no theoretical vagrancy. There is no vacuum. There is no prior assumption. There is no need for political abstractions. It's trendy to label anti-colonialists as a priori Marxists. For my part, I can assure you that my anti- colonialist engagements aren't motivated by class conflict. And I'm not a man with a history. Ibrahim Frantz Fanon, a revolutionary, discovered that what we practice changes our consciousness. You will become a revolutionary if you practice insurrection.

"Why would my subconscious grill me at this stage?" I asked my wife. I explained the Martiniquan Caribbean concept of *dépalé* to her. *Dépalé* isn't just to retract something, say outrageous things, or ramble away on one's deathbed. *Dépalé* means to feel guilty for what one said or did in Martiniquan Caribbean culture – to confess a wrong done to someone through witchcraft. Given how much my Martiniquan Caribbean background influenced me, it had to be what I was doing – dépalé. A marabout was required. Maybe I had a djinn in my room. A few nights ago, I awoke to find a green cloud pulsing near the ceiling in the right corner of my room. It looked like the end of the world to me, and I wanted to run outside to see it all.

Josie, as perceptive as ever and eager to divert my attention away from the cancer cell count, responded that it was most likely related to my illness and what I'd learned since writing *Black Skin, White Mask*. My failure to investigate the role of Arab and African women in the colonial enterprise in depth was due to my lack of knowledge of the struggle at the time. I didn't give women the space they deserved in the struggle because I was influenced by Aimé Césaire's racial consciousness, aka Négritude, which opposes national liberation; and, of course, Martinique and Lyon were not Algeria. *Your criticism of this woman was justified because the decisions she makes encourage the occupation. Mayotte took action against herself and her community. It was a suicidal act. That cannot be rationalized. You are not required to* give her a pass simply because she is a woman.

*Existence comes before essence:*

I thought but didn't tell her that only revolutionary upheavals lift a native out of the despair of surviving as best he or she can under occupation. And after I regained my energy, I told her that what Mayotte said about not knowing what else to do was truthful. After all, her primary concern was overcoming hunger – existence comes before essence. This woman sought to exist in the same way all biological beings must. People who are starving may rebel against their circumstances out of desperation, but they do not start revolutions. National liberation is made up of more than starving natives. Mayotte Capécia had no idea she was a captive of the occupation. Humans are not born omniscient or even informed. But she didn't have time for school. She was too preoccupied with staying one step ahead of starvation.

The European appeal to Mayotte was not solely motivated by the black skin, white mask syndrome or a lack of self-esteem. Surviving a successful and pernicious colonial occupation was at stake. I also had to deal with the issue of women as sexual commodities and sources of power between occupiers and indigenous peoples.

Josie took out her notebook and began writing as she used to.

Mayotte adjusted to her situation with expediency and pragmatism, having to submit to the occupation and endure what tradition says is a woman's place. To achieve essence and develop an anti- colonial deontology, she would need to acquire an identity that would allow her to expand her consciousness and vision in order to challenge tradition. There can be no dialectical progress; no linking to history until that leap is made. Mayotte Capécia had to fulfill her individuality by finding consciousness as a colonial subject. She is stranded without that consciousness. She remains fodder for colonialism, as well as fodder for intellectuals like me to scorn.

How does a poor alienated person, a victim of the occupation, come to question the occupation and join the insurgency? How do natives revolt after over a century of colonial rule? That is where Frantz Fanon erred regarding Mayotte Capecia.

It is not enough to say that life is more difficult for women of color because of the occupation. I had to distinguish between the effectiveness of the occupation in relation to women and the reason why women's lives are made more bitter than men's.

The oncologist visits me once a day, late in the afternoon, to provide me with the cancer cell count. He has a neutral tone of voice and does not appear to be a racist. Racism may be expressed differently in America. Maybe he doesn't need to be one. The white blood cell count is self-explanatory. I don't normally think in such terms, but I'm in America now, and America is synonymous with lynching to express racism. I read about it when I was coming here and saw that 6,500 blacks were lynched here between 1865 and five years ago. (My wife can attest to my reluctance to come here. I would not have allowed it if I did not believe there was more to be done.

There was nothing in my situation that wasn't desperate. I was even desperate to march in the grand parade at the end of the Revolution. I also had some books to write. I was also aware that my usefulness to Algeria had come to an end. And, having seen where the rest of Africa was going, I was eager to use my knowledge of occupier rule and methods as well as my participation in the Algerian war of independence to convince the Africans that decolonizing in accordance with the occupiers' agenda was a fatal mistake. Recognizing that African elites were Africanizing European colonialism didn't help me improve.

How dreadful will Africa's future be? I'm grateful that I won't have to witness the horrors of *coups d'état en série* and dictators for life all over Africa.

The worst place on earth to be dismembered in the manner of the Europeans was Africa. Maybe the Sahara was cursing Africa for being so old and taking the time to create Homo sapiens. Other natural barriers to language distribution, people movement, and commerce did not help Africa prepare for the colonial onslaught. Seeing the Sahara reminded me that Africa is home to one- third of all languages on the planet. What does that tell you? And I wondered to what extent Africa would have been colonialism's preferred destination if not for the Sahara and these other isolation-induced geographical features that have physically shaped Africa. Geographic factors also shape people and cultures. When I saw so much sand, I wondered how much Africa's geographic characteristics contributed to the cultural evolution of the way women are used today and the consequent underdevelopment of the continent. I felt like cursing the Sahara. But I only said merde alors!

These will keep the continent hamstrung for the next hundred years and far beyond. Pan- Africanism is a pipe dream. It's a funnyman who claims otherwise.

Abuse of power will be rampant. Grotesque! The development of infrastructure will be hampered. The game of profiteering will become the game of those in power. Corruption will be endemic, merciless, as will a lack of transparency. Stagnation and decline will be so bad young Africans will have no choice but to escape to Europe, despite Europe's racist gauntlet, in order to get away from Africa's inadequacies.

Agriculture was also not a colonial priority. As a result, Africa has no large-scale farming. If subsistence farming continues on its current scale, Africans will continue to go hungry. There, neocolonialism will have it easy.

I was taken away from my thoughts. This is one of lymphocytic leukemia's side effects. It irritates me, but I have no control over it. Besides, nothing depresses me more than contemplating Africa's future. When my wife is here, I don't treat myself.

When my wife sees tears in my eyes, she knows I'm thinking about Ramdane (Abane) ... Was I naive to believe that revolutionaries are solely concerned with the revolution? Is this why when FLN conspirators assassinated Ramdane I was unable to recover? I remained silent. But everyone knew how I felt. Ramdane was a brother to me. Besides, he was the most strategically astute Mujahedeen in the Algerian uprising. Similar to Lenin in the Russian Revolution. What is a revolution if it doesn't have a rudder? They removed the rudder. What would the revolution be like if there was no architect? They assassinated the architect. The revolution would have been ragged if the Russians had assassinated Lenin, with its left flank in the air, because the Bolsheviks would have been disoriented without their rudder, their most capable and single-minded charismatic architect. The assassination of Ramdane weakened the Algerian revolution's center of gravity, Algeria's political wing, its compass. Ramdane was a visionary who desired that all Algerians take part in the revolution. It never fully recovered.

I was an outsider. I was not born in Algeria. I wasn't even a Muslim. The Kabyls believe that Ramdane was killed because he was a Kabyl. I felt like an outsider after he was murdered. I wrote to escape. If Ramdane were present, I would applaud

Josie's decision to remain in Algeria. Things just aren't the same without Ramdane's political wing as the spearhead of the revolution. Because she is aware of how anxious I am as a result of this, she is able to divert me from my thoughts. Anyhow, I was ruminating on the fact that I was now in America. The American Negro entertainers in France I met in Lyon spoke of their country in lynching terms. With astonishment in their eyes they sang, "Strange fruit hanging from the poplar trees," or something along those lines. They did, however, love France. "Your white man is superior to mine," they joked. If laughter isn't an indication of bitterness, I don't know what is. They admire another racist country because they wish their own was less racist. (I was planning to include this reaction in a paper on colonial escapism.) Why is this the case? They always explain, "We don't get lynched if we're seen with a French woman." Being seen with a white woman and living to tell the tale appears to be the litmus test. In my dissertation, *Black Skin, White Mask,* I wanted to include a chapter about American Negroes in France as part of an examination of racism's responsibility in mental illness and the perceptions racism imposes on us. But since I should be examining how American Negroes are treated in other countries, I skipped that chapter and referred to what I already studied.

White blood cells appear to have increased in comparison to yesterday. However, the last vestige of remission remains. At this point, all I want is for Algeria to be free of colonial rule; to be able to say, "We have freed ourselves." The only way to defeat the occupation was to defeat it. It is the only statement that should pertain to Algeria.

This remission and this thought have energized me a bit. This is an opportunity to consider the mindset of the settler – both the psychological and colonial attitudes that influence his behavior toward the native. I'm thinking about what a wonderful thing a mind is. And what a despicable ruler.

The European colonizer does not descend from above to Africa, the Caribbean, the Middle East, or anywhere else. His arrival isn't an act of charity either. His goal is to exploit the indigenous people, their lands, resources, labor, and so on.

The colonial imperative, "The colony was established for the benefit of France," drives the French settlers to keep marching across indigenous lands.

The settler's goal is to exploit, and he uses exceptional tools to do so. His skin color serves a purpose. Hearing a settler discuss his skin color is akin to hearing someone discuss God.

However, there will never be sufficient settlers in the colony to adequately staff the multiple police forces. So, what incredible secret does he use to pull off this feat? He achieves this by employing the principle of exclusion. He hires *colonisés* to assist him in managing the colony. (*Colonisés*? They are the natives, also known as *Béni-oui- ouis*, who devote their bodies and souls to the occupation. They serve the settlers. The settlers consider them – even call them – *loyal.* They are cannon fodder in the settlers' wars. There is no colonial occupation without the collaboration of the *colonisés*.) The *colonisés* are then elevated to the status of privileged indigènes in colonial societies. They're the first *évolués*. Unfortunately, they are frequently the heirs of what ensues when colonialism enters its official neo-colonial phase. The colonisés operate for the benefit of their immediate families, their extended families, and their ethnic community. They are therefore engaged in activities beneficial to colonialism and harmful to the nation. It is impossible for them to serve the settler and wield a weapon against him at the same time.

The settler, conditioned to be brutal by colonialism's imperative, violently bends the native with rifles and other weapons such as his church to deprive the native of his self- determination. In the face of all of these settler weapons, natives are distorted. They develop *abulia*, a mental illness that deprives them of willpower and the ability to act decisively. There is no colonialism without violence. There is no colonization without native deformations.

To be human, you must first become European. But how do indigenous people become Europeans? It's an impossible task. Any form of rebellion is evidence of African savagery. I was born in Martinique, so I understood how horrifying it was to be regarded as an African savage by the French.

To prove himself worthy of French colonization, the native will pretzel himself, and thousands will volunteer to die in France's wars with Germany. But it's all for naught. (De Gaulle revoked these veterans' allowances two years ago because Algeria had taken up arms in pursuit of liberation.) The occupier is well aware that if he allows the native to become his equal, the colonial system will crumble. Only during the period of transition to official neocolonialism does the occupier engage in pretense. When that happens, it's too late. The native who has not forced the occupier to return his independence remains a leaf in the colonizer's wind.

How the Revolution begins when fear ends. How the Indigène manages to start the process that leads to Algeria's liberation.

Convenience and stress were at the top of the list of anthropological factors influencing how many men volunteered for the insurgency and the Algerian Revolution itself. This raw material, which is cognitive in nature, is essential for comprehending the process that triggered the uprising: The native's ability to regain some sense of consciousness, awareness of himself in relation to the colonial occupation around him, is dependent on his ability to break free from the fear-induced inertia that keeps him undecided in a self-imposed cage, agonizing over whether or not to join the insurgency. There is no prosthesis for indecision paralysis. The native is the one who spins the wheel of his life. It's important to remember that tolerating the occupation is far easier than joining the insurgency. It's more convenient. Volunteering to fight for France is also more convenient. Around 170,000 Algerians sided with France against us. They weren't all Harkis.

The attraction force has a tangible effect on the native's passivity as the colonial authority towers over him in his community and in the bidonvilles, as fear-induced inertia and the inconvenience of joining the insurgency increase exponentially. The strain is unbearable. It becomes a way of life to avoid it. At this point, the native is resigned to his fate and the occupation. The native's ability to break through everything that comes with fear-induced passivity is on trial here, not the native's loyalty to Algeria. (At Blida-Joinville, we had success with adaptive behavior treatments geared toward Algerians joining the uprising in conjunction with panic disorder therapy.) The FLN grew to 300,000 regular enlisted men and nearly 40,000 civilian supporters. Around 100,000 women actively participated in the Revolution.

No one will be prepared for my insights into Algerians' ambivalence about whether or not to join the struggle, or the critical role that stress played in the revolution.

No amount of psychiatric training could have prepared me for the extent to which indigène were willing to tolerate colonial abuse without raising a finger. Likewise, the number of Algerians who fought *against* the Revolution. Stress saps man's resolve, whether in daily life or in joining the Revolution. I believe I spent more time fighting stress evasion at Blida-Joinville than any other type of psychosis. Master stress, if only for a short period, and you'll rule the world.

 *Existential dilemma*:

Ultimately, the French were able to persuade Algerians to remain undecided about their own abuse by persuading them of the pragmatism of collaborating with the colonial authorities. For over a century and a half, this play on natives' indecision contributed to the success of French colonialism. On the other hand, once the native convinced himself that he needed to raise a finger to be free of the occupation, everything conspired to favor his action. Breaking through that fear- induced inertia was the Revolution's most difficult challenge.

When the native's fear-induced inertia is overcome, his demeanor and outlook change. With just one look, you can tell you're in the presence of a Mujahedeen. With his resolve, he has re-established his self- worth. He is brimming with zeal. He has been cured of his psychic akinesia. He is now ablaze with a bright flame, acutely aware of the colonial occupation all around him.

He's impatient, and he's seeking others to join the rebellion. He wants to strengthen the resistance movement he's part of. He has regained his equilibrium. He can now see Algeria achieving self-determination. The end result is a native who has been resurrected both internally and externally. This native is referred to as a redempted native. He is now a threat to the occupation.

On the other hand, if the native does not reclaim his self-awareness and is instead seduced by the ease of doing nothing, he will never be able to take up arms and reclaim his self-determination and self-respect. If the native's passivity isn't a strategic ruse, but rather a dependency; if the occupier sleeps soundly at night, that native remains an accomplice in the colonial enterprise.

With the outbreak of the revolution, occupying settlers intensified their efforts to justify their occupation, claiming, for example, that French colonization of Algeria was simply the restoration of a formerly Christian and Latin territory to its rightful owner. And they spent considerable energy making myths of their actions by quoting from their bibles. The bible always says what you want to hear. The oppressor finds the utility of his oppression there.

Dread is pursuing the settlers. They revive the concept of "native savagery" and live in fear and anxiety – fear of the revolution and unbearable anxiety that the natives will exact personal revenge on them. Until indigenous lands are returned to their rightful owners, fear and anxiety must entrap the occupier in their labyrinths.

When the native's mind is firm, his destination is a firearm, such as the Karabiner 98k or the MAS 36. While the Mujahedeen are fighting on the occupation battlefield, intellectuals like Césaire and Senghor are tearing their hair out trying to figure out how to get their race a seat at the French colonial empire's fanciful *give and take table*, all the while wondering what Paris has in store for them, knowing that French colonialism always has the final say.

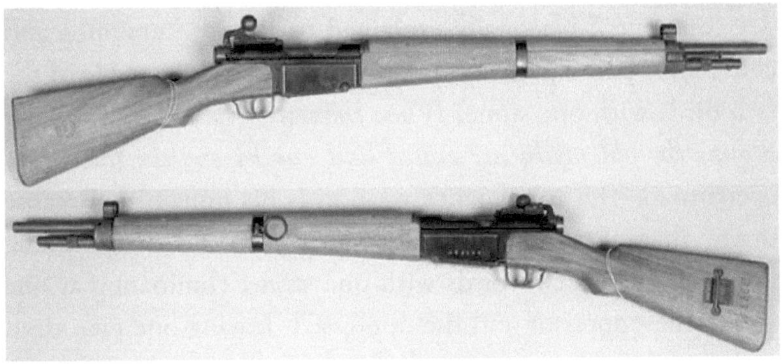

The French MAS-36 rifle was a favorite of the Algerian revolutionaries

The native stands to gain nothing more than further subjugation. Clinically, the occupation is harmful to the native's brain. A high level of stress hormones negatively impacts his behavior. Alienation is a common symptom of mental illness in native communities. Oppressed people are perpetually on the verge of psychic breakdowns. The deranged natives, unable to resist the settler, direct their rage at themselves and their community. They despise themselves in the same way rape victims do. With the outbreak of the insurgency, the occupier has become his target. This gives him freedom. He's devoted to the insurgency His rage is no longer directed at himself or his community. I don't have the data to back this up, but I'm guessing that forensic evidence shows that the revolution significantly reduces the natives' stress hormones. For the occupier, these hormones, of course, work in the opposite direction.

I attempted to convince Africans not to ratify pseudo independences at the expense of self-determination and national development. I personally explained to Patrice Lumumba and conference participants in Africa and Europe the parable of the two birds with one stone: *When the natives put their hands on a gun, the old myths are erased and one by one the taboos* are overturned. The combatant's weapon is his humanity. Because in the first phase of the revolt, murder is a necessity: killing a European kills two birds with one stone, eliminating at one stroke the oppressor and the oppressed: leaving one man dead and the other free.

Colonialism is violence. Without violence, neither occupation nor liberation is possible.

I'm aware that I'm being repetitive. I believe I previously stated that if communists outside the Soviet Union were less rigid, they would have conquered the world. They were doomed by their religious-like inflexibility and subservience to Moscow. I lack the stamina to be succinct. Regardless, I need to move on; it's not as if I have unlimited time. (My wife despises it when I speak in that manner.)

When a native evaluates his situation, he commits a subversive act. He is liberated from his passivity, he's free of inertia and on the path to revolution by his awareness.

 *The firearm as OPEN SESAME:*

As if *A Gun in the Hand of a Native* were a story in *Ali Baba and the Forty Thieves*.

When the Karabiner 98k says *sésame ouvre- toi*, colonialism dissipates like smoke. (When I thought of that, I got *Ali Baba and the Forty Thieves* in a Tunis bookstore after my wife and I were kicked out of my hospital in Blida- Joinville.)

 *The therapeutic appeal of violence:*

What I'm saying is based on personal experience. I was there when the natives first started utilizing violence for their own self-liberation, and I saw personally how much of a game changer that became. Suddenly, the settlers were confronted with a volcano eruption wrapped in a hurricane and an earthquake. And they were scared to death. The more terrified the settlers became, the more courageous the natives became. I recall Julien Bertagnas's remarks. He ruled over the richest vineyards and agricultural lands in the northwest, near Sidi-Bel-Abbés. My hospital purchased geese from one of his farms. I recall him most vividly for his graphic observations about the natives and their firearm activities. He chastised French officials for "allowing natives to terrify his community," telling them, *Ils vont vous traverser comme la merde l'oie.* (They'll go through you like shit through goose.) The rehabilitative power of violence jolted me like an epiphany. I was astounded. It had a mystical quality to it. Transcendental. I simply added a psychiatrist's perspective to that experience. Allow me to reiterate: Colonialism is not rocket science. To a French audience I would translate, *le colonialism n'est pas du tout sorcier.*

The settlers appeared to be giving the native a second look for the first time. Through their occupier's terror, the native had become a human being, a person they could actually see – a case of colon exposure to the new reality. With this game changer, it was clearly a buyer's market. The native no longer acquiesced to colonialism's and European dominance's abuses. He was equipped with a Karabiner 98k. He was no longer just a part of the scenery. I suggested this mantra to my Algerian patients, *I pray with a gun that causes existential fear in the settler's community.*

In that community, a native with a firearm is cause for ontological dread. A prey that has turned against a hunter is an awe- inspiring creature, undeniably. A man who opposes colonial tyranny is unmistakably no longer a colonized man. It's impossible to deny how remarkable this is – a native who is no longer colonized on a rampage against his oppressor. Halleluiah! Catharsized, that native is on a mission to reclaim his land with the same zeal as the Algerian sun. "They're no longer on our side," settlers told me, "and they've guns. They're shooting. They want independence. We thought they wanted us here. How can they rebel against a country that has done everything for them? What can they do without us? They need us."

The bottom line: The game changer is a firearm in the hand of a native:

The settlers' fear of indigène violence frequently leads to psychotic breaks with reality. Overnight, the settlers begin to question the occupation's ethics. What is the cause of this pathology? After so many years of European authority, discovering that the native has become a freedom fighter against them rather than a passive serf is an irreversible shock to the settlers. The inspired Algerian slogan "a suitcase or a coffin" shook the settler communities to the core. A few committed suicide as a result of their shock at losing their sense of superiority, as well as the possibility that the natives would retaliate indiscriminately against the settlers. The settlers became obsessed with the term *indiscriminé* – indiscriminate. The notion that the indigènes would exact "indiscriminate" vengeance against settlers. I found that telling. (I insisted on a *Damned of the Earth* index to detail such mental illnesses.)

I had to explain to those who came to the hospital that the natives were more than just out for vengeance. They wanted their land back more than they wanted reprisals. It was a revolution in the name of Algerian independence, not a boxing match.

Humanism in the twentieth century is anti- colonialism. There isn't a day that goes by that I don't recite the first few lines of Sartre's Black Orpheus. I'd occasionally use them to ask settlers, "What did you expect?" What were you hoping for when you removed the gag that was keeping these mouths shut? That they would extol your virtues? Did you expect to see adoration in the eyes of these heads that your fathers and you forced to bend down to the ground when they stood up again? I love Sartre's questions to colonists ... So to the point. So appropriate for a rising revolution. Such assertive questions abound in literature.

I also like Shakespeare's to wrong the wrongdoer till he render right. Alternatively, the unjust sinned until the unjust was corrected. To the delight of my FLN colleagues, I recited them numerous times.

Tell me who the settlers are, and I'll tell you how racist they are toward the natives. It wasn't until I read Sartre's *Anti-Semite and Jew* that I realized *where* the settlers' racism came from and how much their low self- esteem contributed to the brutality we've all witnessed toward the natives. Look into what Sartre discusses in *Anti-Semite and Jew* if you want to understand one of the primary etiologies of colonialism. Sartre's statement about anti-Semitism captivated me, and I memorized it for future reference: Anti- Semitism brings more than just the pleasure of hating; it also brings positive pleasures. By portraying the Jew as a deplorable and pernicious being, I simultaneously affirm that I am a member of the elite ... There is nothing I can do to earn my superiority, and nothing I can do to lose it. It is given once and for all ... anti- Semitism is a poor man's snobbery.

Upper class plantation owners in the southern states of the United States referred to their poor white brethren as "white trash," distinguishing them from the upper layers of cotton plantation society. Poor whites were the most anti-black, motivated by class snobbery and cognitive animosity toward blacks. The plantation owners knew what they were doing when they hired them as overseers. The colonial authorities employ the services of like-minded settlers to maintain control over the natives. These impoverished white settlers expect to be rewarded and advanced up the colonial social ladder. However, even within occupations, one class's.dominance can only be based on the degradation of another. When poor white settlers are still rejected by the established colonial classes, they become bitter Europeans, and their psychological disorders spread throughout the colony. They are in desperate need of a salve to relieve their psychological letdown. They find it in their hatred for the natives – in their lower-class snobbery. This has an impact on all colonial behaviors.

In France, nationalism and economic interests compel the bourgeoisie and middle classes to back the country's colonial endeavors. France is a second-class nation without its colonies, trailing only Belgium and Portugal. France, on the other hand, is on par with Britain and Germany due to its imperial holdings. Besides, imperialism boosts the French bourgeoisie's confidence and arrogance. It is a source of bourgeois pride.

The Europeans who became colonist settlers, of course, did not come from this bourgeoisie. They came from the lower classes; some were criminals or deportees, mostly from France but also from southern Europe, especially Spain, Italy, Malta and were encouraged by France to increase the number of white settlers in Algeria and maintain its stranglehold on the country. When I practiced in Algeria, there were over a million permanent settlers. Additionally, France had declared Algeria to be an inalienable part of France.

The process of colonialism accelerated when they targeted Algerians and Africans for exploitation. Brutality was the norm, and they ignored moral principles. They did not impose colonial laws and customs haphazardly. These laws and customs were precise, pinpoint precise. The colonizers' goal was to make the indigène as dependent on them as possible as quickly as possible. Then European imperialism was naturalized. Then formalized into laws, along with their racial caste system.

The indigènes struggled to adjust to the conditions of their occupation. They were able to survive by making psychological adjustments. Their level of blind hope astounded me. That kind of hope demands nothing from the world's wretched. But it's an exercise in passivity. Be clear about one thing: if the native's only chance of surviving is to hold on to hope, then he's stuck. He won't be able to advance until his Karabiner 98k is pointed in the direction of the occupier. This is the only chance he has of surviving successfully.

Despair can also be a source of renewal. We gave birth to the revolution, to ourselves, and to the Algerian nation, out of despair.

Settlers found a privileged status and superiority under colonial rule, ruling over millions of natives. The European have-nots were reborn in the colonies. Colonialism became their religion. The colonial system had no more devout worshipers. With a demonic obsession, the grasping settlers protected their racial privileges.

Colonialism is like a religion. The colonialists want the subjugated to accept their condition at all costs. Unless the natives claim their personal inferiority and that of their culture, they are considered disloyal inferiors. You are dominated because you are inferior. You have to accept it. You have to show it. It is that simple. There is no reverse of this coin.

You can count on the settler petty bourgeois to follow the pattern that protects them from their lower class status and increases their self-esteem. Under their dominion, the indigènes became the wretched of the earth. However, these poor whites are burdened with psychological impediments that result in a variety of cognitive biases against natives. Fatalism is ingrained in their communities as if by reflex; for somewhere in the back of their collective minds is the understanding that they do not deserve their privileged status. It can't last forever. The right of conquest is a myth, and they are right to be nervous about the natives becoming resentful and even violent. Their sense of insecurity grows stronger, driving them to be more cruel to the indigènes.

As much as violence against the settlers liberates the natives, it also subjects the settlers to a state of constant fear – a diligent companion. The settlers are desperate to hold on and are constantly demanding that apartheid's parameters be tightened. During the war, they backed fascists. This group's intellectuals – men like Albert Camus – pretzel themselves to create a make-believe world of sunshine, gentle breezes, and inviting Algerian beaches. Mediterraneanism is the name of that world; it is their fictitious Mediterranean culture.

These settlers are trapped in the part of their identity that is based on hatred and racism toward the indigènes. They will never be able to break free. Apartheid is their only safe haven. There is no room for moral principles there. Algeria's Pieds Noirs are one example. To keep the colony in line, the colonial administration takes advantage of their insecurity and need to maintain control over the natives and the land. This adds another layer of oppression and brutality to the lives of the natives. Then the colonial administration celebrates 'the French colonizing genius' and congratulates itself. On the other hand, the Pieds Noirs want absolute guarantees that the Algerians will not force France to return Algeria to its natives. The Pieds Noirs want the natives in certain places but not others. Algeria must become an apartheid state. The demands of the Pieds Noirs overthrew France's fourth republic, pushing France to the brink of bankruptcy and disintegration.

The concept of "poor man's snobbery" Sartre refers to prevails in this group of European settlers. It does in ways that even the colonial administration considers offensive, such as ensuring natives are degraded in the belief that it strengthens the occupation. Anxious "Ultra" settlers kept a close eye on Algerians. It was acceptable to abuse the Algerians because they were rats. Animalization is a form of racism and a sign of colonialism. Ratonnades – the killing of rats – were tasked with putting an end to Algerian nationalism. Ratonnades hate crimes replaced military sweeps in Kasbah assaults.

These settlers also appeared to derive "positive pleasures" from destroying the natives' properties, with a particular fondness for uprooting the Kabyles's olive trees. One settler told me that olive trees symbolized Christianity and that they should not be grown on land not under European control. The settlers' infliction of as much suffering as they can upon the worthless natives is a clear metaphor for colonialism.

Not all settler petty bourgeois are uneducated. Albert Camus was not uneducated, and he was a deservedly eminent writer.

His *Myth of Sisyphus* is a masterwork. A man who said, "I rebel, therefore I exist," knows what it's all about. But not enough to see beyond his European origins and support a free Algeria. He criticized our reaction to the ratonnades and called it an "excuse."

Likewise Aimé Césaire and many other intellectuals, Camus prefers reforming colonialism over eradicating it, just like an oncologist would ameliorate a cancer instead of beating it. Sartre was correct in his assessment of Camus.

Another bout of epistaxis.

The last remission appears to have ended. I suspect it is the last. I was even able to walk during this remission. I'm not going to walk again. My thoughts are jumbled. I'm hoping I don't lose them completely. I wanted to glance at the issue of development once the armed phase of the revolution is over.

*Above all women!*

I should have considered the role of women in the Algerian Revolution, and not just because they dressed in western garb to transport weapons around Algiers and the Kasbahs. Approximately 100,000 women actively supported the Revolution.

What will their life be like after the revolution? I should have asked. Will Islamic tradition be arbitrarily reaffirmed in order to deny them fundamental rights? I Frantz Fanon squandered a life-changing opportunity to point out that without firm guarantees of equal rights for women, Algeria will flounder, trapped in the mother of all dead ends – men's self-serving tradition. This means that despite triumphing in one of the world's seminal liberation struggles, over a century of servitude and insults will continue. Stagnation will emerge as the ultimate victor. Yes, a culture of stagnation will set in if we allow mindless traditions to continue destituting women. Algeria's progress will be stifled until that's addressed. Women will be on the cutting edge of innovation once they have been liberated. Liberation is the mother of all innovation?

The inherent human drive to do away with anything that hurts us is innate in women too – be it a toothache or an oppressor. They'll be included if we stick to our revolutionary principles. After all, if the last is not first, what is a revolution? "If you want to know what a revolution is, call it progress." I think it's Victor Hugo who said that. However, if we find inconveniences in the progress of their liberation, the revolution will be a sad exploit, indeed.

Roberto Holden paid me a visit. I'm too far gone to remember what I said to him. However, I am sure I repeated what I said a thousand times before - defeat your occupation. And I must have mentioned that the Karabiner 98k accomplished the unthinkable in Algeria. I always do. As liberation and subservience cannot be equated, there can be no doubt about what the native must do to reclaim nationhood.

Oppose the occupation. Eradicate it completely.

Not only does armed struggle lead to self- determination, but it'll also gives Algerians the once-in-a-lifetime vitality necessary to manage the burden of national development that the country must live through after French colonialism and a war of independence. That vitality comes only from a successful Revolution. It's the rarest thing in the world.

Do not sit at a table with the Portuguese until independence is secured. Follow Amilcar Cabral, Guinea-Bissau's Ramdane Abane. Regrettably, the list with names like Cabral and Ramdane is the world's shortest. Cabral is the only leader outside of Algeria who fully grasps the concept of nationhood. And Cabral understands the significance of the gun in liberating the native's psyche. But he also values culture, understanding that national liberation entails more than just armed struggle. Culture is what proves one's nation, not merely that a culture exists, but how it manifests itself in the struggle for nationhood against colonial forces.

In Europe, without African colonies, colonialism is the "snobbery of the poor" for the Portuguese and Belgians that anti-Semitism is for the lower classes of which Sartre speaks. This means they will fight to the death to keep these settlements in Africa. The Portuguese are impoverished, but South Africa and the United States support them. It will be difficult to get Portugal out of Africa. Holden should abandon his tribalism and focus on Angola's national liberation by working to unite all insurgent groups in Africa opposed to Portuguese colonialism. Tribalism! Yes, it provides some solace. However, it's the curse of multiethnic nations. "I'd like to stereotype you before you stereotype me." That's the tribal mindset. It's a recipe for ethnic strife. Tribalism has proved it's colonialism's best friend.

Tribal bonds shape the economic and sociopolitical structure of Africa. People are zealous in defending their tribal identities. Politicians and other con artists, on the other hand, use tribal identities to defraud the public and introduce them to the culture of corruption. Tribalism is the Damocles' Sword that hangs over Africa's development.

No one with a tribal mindset should lead a liberation movement. Forget about the Congo. Lumumba's assassination sealed the Congo's fate. He gained notoriety as a result of the manner in which he was assassinated. Lumumba made the mistake of believing, too quickly, that he could achieve independence without defeating the occupation's establishment, which was already plotting the dismemberment of the Congo. Lumumba had no idea what to do with the independence granted to him by the colonialists because Belgium was already way ahead of him, with a stranglehold on Katanga and all its commodities.

Peaceful decolonization is enticing, undoubtedly. The problem is that it wouldn't be peaceful if neo-colonialism wasn't already in place. It's a cover up. It is of the utmost importance for the people of Africa to attain their independence in a fashion that is antagonistic toward neocolonialism. Not by signing a piece of paper in front of a crowd and King Baudouin, but by being hostile to colonialism. I'm not arguing that it should always be done the way the Viet Minh did it in Indochina or the Algerians did it in North Africa. You might think I'm a fool. You must know, though, that natives enter the next stage of colonialism with one hand tied behind their backs unless they pay for their freedom with struggle currency.

The pursuit of liberation through persuasion is motivated more by its inherent complexity than by the fact that it is simple. Because it purifies, convincing liberation purges the nation of most of the traces of colonialism. If the nation does not have the benefit of a fresh start after colonialism, what other option does it have but to remain a vassal of the colonial power?

As Lumumba's murder demonstrates, the independence granted to him by the Belgians was not worth the parchment it was written on – it was a colonialist independence, not a native one.

If the native did not commandeer his liberation but is released by the *colon*, he remains bound to the occupation. There's a world of difference between colonialism acting on you and you acting on yourself. I am convinced it's preferable to remain under colonialist control until the revolution than to do what Lumumba did. Revolution is not for parchment, not until the Karabiner 98k has had its way with generations of colonial authority and restored the native to his rightful place – not until the last is first.

Only Algeria had what it took to defeat the occupation in Africa the way it should be defeated. Truces are snares. We must not agree to a cease-fire until the country's independence is ratified.

*Hypoxemia and hemorrhages:*

In response to the hypoxemia, a nasal cannula is inserted into my nose. The cause was cerebral hypoxia. The extra oxygen has given me a boost. It's like a tonic, and I'm less agitated as a result. The earlier hemorrhages appear to be less severe.

What were you thinking? Of course, the French. The French will do their damnedest to show that the Chinese Communists, the Egyptians, who knows? deceived the Algerians. They'll claim that France was about to grant us full equality and spend whatever it took to turn Algeria into a paradise.

Look how enraged De Gaulle became when Sékou Touré told him to his face that Guinea preferred freedom in poverty to opulence in slavery. And consider what De Gaulle did to the Guineans after they voted for independence. Then too, two years ago, De Gaulle and his Army Minister Pierre Mesmer froze the pensions of Algerian veterans who fought and died for France. Settlers do not relinquish their occupation gracefully. The majority of them are petty bourgeoisie, prey to the small mind. They rush to racism, as well as all forms of mutilation and vengeance at the first opportunity. French expats in West Africa went so far as to form the National Liberation Front of Guinea in order to reclaim Guinea in the name of colonialism. How much harsher will they be toward us now that we have won a full-fledged revolution against them and forced De Gaulle to bow to the evidence that the occupation had failed in Algeria?

How many Algerian colonial fronts are they going to open against us? Guinea is a foreshadowing. They attempted to destabilize it by beggaring the Guinean people, expecting them to go on strike and force Sékou Touré to take extralegal measures to protect the country and his rule. He did, in fact. Sékou Touré is not made of what is required to withstand such a colonial ambush. He thinks that plastering the country with trivial slogans incite revolutions. He intends to use the attacks against him to isolate the country in order to maintain his rule and become a dictator. In doing so, he will demonstrate the colonizer's case. It is 1961, and he has already established the authoritarian state of Guinea, with the Democratic Party of Guinea serving as the sole legal party. Fortunately, he has Ghana's Kwame Nkrumah to steady him. I'm familiar with Nkrumah. He made an attempt to teach me English. He recognizes the superiority of armed struggle in liberating Africa. He carries Africa's hope on his shoulders.

*Irregular breathing - reflective:*

Will my Algerian brothers be prepared for the onslaught of the petty-bourgeoisie? We should brace ourselves for them to do to us what they did to the Guineans times ten. They're going to blow up facilities in order to deprive Algeria of basic services, and they're going to try to bring us down economically. We should prepare by stockpiling water and food to withstand the impending offensive. We must also protect Jews, Pieds- Noirs and Harkis from retaliation, lest the French massacre our people to discredit us. These settlers and their collaborators will be desperate to flee, fearing that the Algerians will do to them what they did to the Algerians. Before treaties are signed, we should grant them Algerian nationality. They, too, were victims of the occupation. Also, keep in mind that they include specialists and skilled workers among them. It would be an understatement to say that Algeria is in desperate need of specialists and skilled workers. It's reassuring that nativism was never a part of Algerian culture.

With self-interest and De Gaulle's personal feelings toward "Arabs" on their side, the forces of neocolonialism will circle over us like vultures circling a rare desert antelope, doing everything they can to demonstrate how misguided we were in waging war for self-determination, and how much better Algeria was under French occupation.

I am also concerned about the rise of last- minute converts to the insurgency, parasites masquerading as mujahedeen fighters. This type of defector is common wherever there is a conflict. They're the *croque-morts* of a war's end. The Revolution outsiders. They'll assassinate Harkis or any other easy target to prove their mujahedeen credentials. They are evil and have the potential to cause irreparable harm to the revolution. They must be mercilessly eliminated.

The liberation of Algeria will have what effect on my Algerian brothers?:

Liberation will restore Algeria's birthright to self-governance and secure our future independence, but it won't erase Algeria's colonial past. This isn't deliverance. It won't, for example, erase the psychological legacy of ratonnades and the other atrocities committed to keep Algeria under French rule. Revolutions do not work like magic wands. Furthermore, revolutions have a cursed proclivity to betray themselves. Then too, humility will help people to appreciate the fact that they have been given a once-in-a-lifetime opportunity to reform society. A revolutionary transformation! That's what's needed.

Will the Algerian National Liberation Army relinquish control following its victory? Or will the army cling to power behind a single man or a junta? In the latter case, all national resources will be devoted to keeping that man and the army in power. How much money will be left over for national development? Is Algeria going to be the next Guinea? I hope this never happens.

If – I repeat, if – the National Liberation Army maintains control, the story will be tragic: The head of state will live in constant fear of a coup by one of his comrades. "If I can stage a coup, why can't another general?" will be his fearful mantra. Only coups would bring about change, with all of the consequences that entails in extra-judicial measures. Repressive legislations will be enacted as quickly as the stooping falcon I once saw in the desert. Turmoil will follow. Algeria will be consumed by it. I will die fearing for the safety of my wife in Algeria if the FLN Revolution leaders monopolize power following the Revolution.

There is an alternative. Algeria must not become another Guinea. The National Liberation Army must do what Ramdane Abane died for: Allow civilians – real civilians, not military men in suits – to assume ultimate responsibility in Algeria and establish a functioning government. That, of course, is what would make sense. Accepting a real government would be the sophisticated, proper, and beneficial conclusion to the revolution – and, without a doubt, the most advantageous to national development. If the army retains control, the world will forget the great Algerian Revolution in a few years, remembering only the ignominious conclusion of the Revolution's spectacle of the colonel's or general's seizure of power. We will be ashamed rather than proud.

We can always hope for the best. We can hope that those who rely on hope will not go hungry forever.

Algerians will wonder why we sacrificed so much for nationhood if the opportunity to replace French colonialism with a non-rivalrous and non-excludable socio- political system is not eagerly embraced. As nationhood struggles to establish itself, the revolution will become a reference point, and De Gaulle will have his day. Furthermore, we must not be misled into thinking that just because the French are burdened by De Gaulle's view that France must let us go to remain "European," they are done with us. De Gaulle reeks of vengeance. He will not take lightly the fact that the Algerian Revolution precipitated the disintegration of the French empire in Africa, and that Kabyles, Berbers, and Arabs imposed their liberation on him, forced themselves on France, and released Algeria with their blood and revolution.

The French state was on the verge of civil war and destruction as a result of France's insane determination to keep a lost Algeria. Forget? France or De Gaulle will never forget the Algerian revolution. I worked as a psychiatrist. Here in this hospital room number 37, on this deathbed, on December 6, 1961, I'm telling you that they'll never forget.

Some African French leaders, such as Houphouet-Boigny and Leopold Senghor, share De Gaulle's sentiments. Our Revolution shattered their dream of remaining under French rule. The Algerian revolution inspired people all over the world. My last smile came when I heard that de Gaulle reminded Senghor that the French are "a European people of the white race, Greek and Latin culture, and Christian religion." When my FNL colleagues heard this, they died laughing. Senghor's hatred for Algeria was unfathomable.

When writing about women in colonial conditions, I should have remembered dear Josie. What happens to her after the revolution? She said she would not return to Lyon. She intended to stay in Algeria. Would my name be enough to ensure her and my son's safety?

 *Without Ramdane there is no guarantee:*

When Ramdane Abane was assassinated, it was clear that Algeria was fighting more than just the French occupation. Why make things easy for the insurgents? Why should Algeria be distinguished from the rest of Africa? As the revolution will not provide Algeria with magical armor to protect it from the legacy of colonialism, the revolution will almost certainly not serve as a deterrent to its participants. Rivalries and aspirations will stain the revolution. We'd like to think that being a part of the revolution made us virtuous, but that's misinterpreting men.

Another case of pneumonia was diagnosed: To die like this in America ... what a waste. It's painful to die here when I could have done so three months ago on the decolonization battlefield.

This day's twilight ... Algeria, the occupation, and dreadful colonialism That's what it was all about. The "Algerian" who fights for his humanity and the "Algerian" who died for his liberation.

At the door, there's a coma: I see Fort de France ... In La Savane, a gleaming flamboyant tree blooms. I used to sit under that tree as a boy, daydreaming about my mother's red snapper court bouillon dinner.

Josie, I adore you.

As long as occupations exist, there'll be a Fellagha named Frantz Fanon ... A Fellagha to oppose the colonial curse ...

As dusk approaches, I am reminded of the Algerian and third-world people who are under occupation. I persisted for the sake of them. When you pass by my grave, please say aloud, "The man lying here was a Fellagha, an enemy of colonialism. He fought in the Algerian revolution."

Tomb of Frantz Fanon, Cemetery of the martyrs, Aïn Karma, Algeria. On the tomb is written in Arabic "Doctor Ibrahim Frantz Fanon"

1.189e jour de la Révolution Algérienne

LA RÉVOLUTION PAR LE PEUPLE ET POUR LE PEUPLE

EL MOUDJAHID

Organe Central du Front de Libération Nationale Algérienne

Numéro 17
1er février 1958
Prix : 30 francs

EDITORIAL

L'O.N.U. doit intervenir

LA CROIX ROUGE INTERNATIONALE FACE A LA GUERRE D'ALGERIE

RESURRECTION NATIONALE ET REVOLUTION DEMOCRATIQUE

LIRE EN PAGE

El Moudjahid, Fanon's newspaper while he was in Tunisia

Josie Fanon

Mme Josie Fanon made these remarks to the author at Howard University's African- American Center on November 16, 1978.

On July 13, 1989, Josie Fanon committed suicide in El Biar, Algers. She was laid to rest in Algers' El Kettar cemetery. She was 58 years old and was born Marie-Joseph Dublé in Lyon, France.

cf: What is the purpose of your visit to the United States this year?

Fanon, Josie: I returned this year on the invitation of the United Nations Special Committee Against Apartheid, which is organizing a series of homages and commemorations to black revolutionaries throughout the year, most notably Paul Roberson, Nelson Mandela of the A.N.C., President Nkrumah, and others. The committee decided to pay tribute to Frantz in this context and invited me.

cf: How do you feel about your second trip to America?

Fanon, Josie: Personally, I am a bit shaken to be back in the United States because it's where my husband died. I'm also interested in observing black civil rights movements in the United States, examining new perspectives, and discussing what the future holds.

cf: You previously visited the United States in 1961. When exactly were you here in 1961, and what brought you here?

Fanon, Josie: I came to the United States in November 1961 because my husband was being treated at the National Institutes of Health Bethesda Hospital. The Algerian Provisional Government (APG) brought him here for medical treatment. Doctors diagnosed him with leukemia a year earlier while he was representing Algeria's provisional government in Ghana. They initially sent him to Moscow for treatment, but the disease worsened, and the APG, with the assistance of the Tunisian government, approached the Americans for assistance. They believed that the best medical facilities were in the United States at the time. He came to the United States under these circumstances.

However, you should be aware that he did not arrive here of his own volition. In fact, he was opposed to this solution. He was hesitant to travel to the United States because he was a black man, a militant, and an anti-imperialist revolutionary fighter. But he really didn't have a choice. He was gravely ill, and he was on the verge of death.

cf: As we passed through the campus gate, you told me that your son, Olivier, had attended Howard University in 1961. Could you elaborate on that?

Josie Fanon: My son was a toddler at the time, and because I had to care for my husband – I was here for more than a month – I visited Frantz every day and spent many nights with him in the hospital. We enrolled our young son in Howard University's kindergarten at the time.

cf: what is your current occupation?

Josie Fanon: I've been a professional journalist for a while now. I worked for the Algerian press from 1962, the year of Algeria's independence, until last year [1977]. I also worked in the information section with the Algerian Front for National Liberation. Since 1977, I've worked for *Demain L'afrique/ Tomorrow Africa*, a Pan- African magazine published monthly in Paris. I moved to Paris for that reason.

cf: How did Frantz Fanon meet you?

Josie Fanon: I met him in Lyon (in the southeast of France). We were both students. My major was liberal arts, while his was medicine. We met at a theater. When we met, he was 23 and I was 18.

cf: Speaking of Lyon, would you be willing to retrace Fanon's life for us?

Josie Fanon: Frantz had been in France for about four years when I met him. Understand that he was from Martinique; having been born in a French colony, he had assimilated all of France's cultural values. This pathology is common among the French-speaking people of the Antilles. Even today, these are the territories

where French colonialism has been most over-emphasized, perfidious, and noxious. During the Second World War, Frantz, who was still very young at the time, joined the Free French Forces. This meant that he identified with France for a time. However, after visiting France and confronting French society's racism, he began to comprehend and analyze his own and his countrymen's experiences. This analysis resulted in the publication of *Black Skin, White Mask* in 1952. He was twenty-five years old at the time.

He was also a medical student specializing in psychiatry at the time. After finishing his studies, he planned to return to the Antilles or Africa to look for work. He couldn't get a job in Martinique, Guadeloupe, or Senegal for administrative reasons, so he chose Algeria, which was still in Africa. This was in 1953, a year before the Algerian revolutionary armed struggle began. He had already made contact with Algerian nationalists, so he was already a part of the revolutionary movement when the revolution began. Nothing here is surprising. Many people wonder why Fanon went to Algeria or what kind of relationship a man from Martinique could have had with Algeria.

The answer is straightforward: There is a fundamental fraternity between all colonized people and people colonized by the same foreign power. Fanon was not unfamiliar with the Algerian revolution. In 1957, the French government expelled us from Algeria. We went to Tunisia, where the Front for National Liberation had an external branch and later formed the Provisional Government of the Algerian Revolution.

Fanon was a member of the F.N.L. and the Provisional Government. He was also interested in the dissemination of news. They appointed him as the Provisional Government's Ambassador to Accra in 1960. We can retrace Fanon's steps. From his situation as an individual under French rule to his consciousness as a black man through his experience in a colonial society – up to a superior level and his commitment to the larger cause of the Algeria Revolution and, on a higher level, the African Revolution in general.

Fanon had already participated in a number of African people's conferences prior to his appointment as ambassador to Accra, including the first one in 1958. During the conference, he met with other African leaders of the time, including Patrice Lumumba, Felix Moumié of Cameroon, and President Kwame Nkrumah of Ghana. His field of experience and action widened, leading to the writing of *The Wretched of the Earth.*

cf: Ramdane Abane's death was one of the vicissitudes of the Algerian revolution. According to what I've read, your husband was close to him. I'm curious because there's a lot of writing about Ramdane right now. He is widely regarded as the architect of the Algerian revolution. He was assassinated by members of the National Liberation Front.

Josie Fanon: Yes, Franz was deeply influenced by Abane, not only because he was one of the revolution's architects, but also because he understood that all Algerians needed to be involved in the struggle for the sake of Algeria's future after the Revolution. Colonial society is irreparable. With the dominant ethnic and French colonial systems, there could be no compromise. Aside from that, he was opposed to chaos in any form – actions or ideas. The only solution was to liberate Algeria by force of arms. Abane and Franz were of the same mind, realizing that only a national liberation conflict could free Algeria. Furthermore, he insisted on the political branch being superior to the military. This is what he was aiming for. To say the least, his death was a shock. Frantz struggled to recover from his death. I'll leave it at that.

cf: Do you know what Fanon's plans were after *The Wretched of the Earth* was published?

Josie Fanon: It's impossible to say what Fanon would have done if he hadn't died when he did. Two things were constantly changing in his life. He would undoubtedly have continued his political activities. However, I am unable to pinpoint a specific location. He would have stayed in Algeria, no doubt – at least for a while. He fought for its independence and because Algeria was a country close to his heart. This is exactly what I've done. His scientific interests were also an important consideration. He was a psychiatrist who had never given up on his studies in that or other medical fields. Even though he was involved in politics and writing, he always practiced medicine.

cf: He was not what you'd call a professional revolutionary then.

Josie Fanon: He wasn't a professional revolutionary, that's for sure. He was a man who was very open to reality. In fact, he based everything he wrote on personal experiences rather than abstract theories.

cf: How would you evaluate Fanon's work since his death in the context of recent African history?

Josie Fanon: Everything that has happened in Africa since its independence in 1960-1962 demonstrates the accuracy of Fanon's viewpoints. People who are oppressed or colonized can only be freed through armed struggle. That was the case with the Portuguese colonies, and it is the case with what is currently happening in South Africa. How can a negotiated solution for majority rule be found there? Conflicts in Zimbabwe, South Africa, and Namibia in recent years have demonstrated this. It is an illusion and a trick to believe that blacks can achieve majority rule in that country through a negotiated solution. Africans in that region of the continent will have to fight a long and protracted armed conflict. Furthermore, I do not believe they will be successful without the support of the black American people.

cf: Can you tell us about Fanon's friendship with the Négritude poets, Aimé Césaire and Leon Damas?

Josie Fanon: Fanon was Césaire's student in Martinique. Césaire, Damas, and others like them were crucial in his intellectual evolution in terms of his awareness of his own négritude. He held high regard for Césaire and Damas. Nonetheless, he had already realized that, politically, Césaire could have done a lot more for Martinique's independence. Independence is a requirement for political freedom. Even when neocolonialism is not officially active in a country, it is preferable to occupation and total dependence. National liberation is an organic first step; without it, very little can be done. Nation building cannot begin without independence.

cf: What is the colonial situation in Fanon's birthplace, the French-speaking Antilles?

Josie Fanon: Conditions in Martinique were not as clear when Fanon left as they are now. He couldn't stop thinking about

Martinique. I believe he would be more concerned today, because Martinique, Guadeloupe, and Guyane are simply French colonies with a different name. I believe he would devote his entire energy to the service of his country (Martinique) and the Caribbean region as a whole.

cf: The second chapter of Black Skin, White Mask is devoted to Mayotte Capecia, the pseudonym of Lucette Ceranus from Carbet in Martinique. She passed away in 1955. Did Fanon have a personal relationship with her? She exemplifies Fanon's disapproval in *Black* Skin, White Mask.

Josie Fanon: I've heard a lot of different things about Mayotte Capecia and what Frantz said about her in *Black Skin, White Mask*. Her books became well known as a result of Frantz. Frantz is not interested in Mayotte. He was all too aware of the colonial realities of his birthplace. He was well aware that there was little chance of Martinique emerging from the colonial quagmire. Mayotte Capecia was one of the many penalties imposed by the occupation. He fully comprehended what Mayotte – a woman of color living under extreme colonialism – had to endure in order for her family to survive. Her books, *Je Suis Martiniquaise* and *La Négresse Blanche*, on the other hand, were insidious propaganda that praised self-hatred and colonial occupation. Even without that, Frantz examined a pathology characterized by abnormal and dysfunctional effects resulting from psychological disorders common during colonial occupation. We must not lose sight of the fact that we are dealing with a pathology designed to turn natives into apologists for the occupation. Frantz worked as a therapist. He was investigating psychopathologies. His interest in this particular colonial pathology was nothing out of the ordinary.

cf: Jean Paul Sartre prefaced *The Wretched of the Earth* when it was published. Sartre's preface is removed in subsequent editions. Why?

Josie Fanon: Sartre's preface to *The Wretched of the Earth* was removed at my request. Let us say that it is a good preface from a Western perspective. In *The Wretched of the Earth*, Sartre grasped the subject matter. However, when Israel declared war on the Arab countries in June 1967, there was a huge pro-Zionist movement in favor of Israel among western (French) intellectuals. Sartre was a participant in this movement. He signed petitions in support of Israel. His pro- Zionist views, I felt, were incompatible with Fanon's work. Whatever Sartre's previous contributions were, the fact that he did not understand the Palestinian problem reversed his previous political positions.

cf: Much has been written about Fanon. What is your reaction if you have kept up with what has been written?

Josie Fanon: Many Western intellectuals have written about Fanon. They haven't fully grasped his works, in my opinion. There is still a lot to be said. However, I believe that valid Fanon research will be conducted in Africa and in the African-American community in the United States.

cf: Some critics argue that there is a fundamental contradiction between Fanon's works, what he stood for, and his marriage to a white French woman. How do you respond to these critics?

Josie Fanon: It is my opinion, and I believe it was also his – otherwise, he would not have contracted or remained in this interracial marriage. In his works, he states unequivocally that understanding and resolving racial issues requires a revolutionary process. Otherwise, we end up in dead-end situations that are impossible to resolve – the kind that we will never be able to put to rest. Critics can, for example, accuse a black American of marrying an Arab woman because her skin is lighter than his, and so on. In a certain stage of the struggle, such a position can have a positive and beneficially unifying effect for a period of time. However, it is still a limitation. We're not going to limit ourselves to race! Where, then, is the revolution? We can draw a parallel between such personal issues and Fanon's concept of Négritude. Négritude, in his opinion – and this was later proven to be correct – was merely a stage in the dialectical process of the black man's struggle for liberation. END

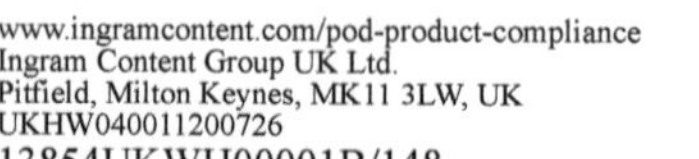

www.ingramcontent.com/pod-product-compliance
Ingram Content Group UK Ltd.
Pitfield, Milton Keynes, MK11 3LW, UK
UKHW040011200726
13854UKWH00001B/148

9 798215 295274